Cookbook Th... ...

Make You Feel Like John Wick

Irresistible and Simple Recipes That Will Bring You Closer to the Real Action

by

Betty Green

Copyright © 2021 by Betty Green. All Rights Reserved.

Copyright/License Page

This book is under a license which means no one is allowed to print a copy, republish it or sell it. Also, you are not allowed to distribute the content from inside this book. The only one who has permission to do these things is the author. If you came across an illegal copy of this book please deleted it immediately, if possible contact us and get the legal version.

This is a book for information and the author won't take any responsibility for the actions that the reader takes following this info. The author has done his part to check that everything inside the book is accurate. So every step that the reader follows must be done with caution.

Table of Contents

Introduction 6

Hot-Like-John Wings 8

Wick-ed Tuna Casserole 10

The Elder's Potato Mash... 12

Hitman's potato salad 14

The Bogeyman's Brownies... 16

The Assassin's pie 18

The Bowery King's Salmon Salad 20

Bogeyman's style brisket.. 22

The Continental Pimiento Cheese Spread.. 24

Wick-y Chicken 25

Wick Potatoes... 27

The High Table's Clam Chowder... 29

Daisy's Special 31

The Adjudicator's pudding 33

Sweet Like John Cream Pie 35

Wick's Casserole 37

Baba Yaga's Collard Greene 39

Wick and beans 41

The High Table Chicken Enchilada Casserole 43

Baba Yaga's Rice 45

The Continental Fried Okra 47

John's Hash 49

Bowery King's Gelatin Salad 51

The Hitman's Chicken Enchiladas 53

Wick's Brunswick Stew 55

Heavy Duty Ham 57

The Adjudicator Style Cobbler 59

The Elder's Macaroni and Cheese 61

Hitman's Hash 63

Continental Hotel Apple Pie 65

Excommomunicado Jambalaya 67

John's Sloppy Joes 69

Wick Style Cheese Soup 71

Bogeyman's Buckeye 73

Wick n Peas 75

The High Table Potato Salad 77

Baba Yaga's noodle soup 79

John's Okra and Chicken Gumbo 82

The Bogeyman's Funeral Potatoes 85

Parabellum-Style Ribs...87

The Continental Onion Dip........... 89

The Continental Salad 90

Bowery King's Stuffed Salmon....................................... 93

Baba Yaga's Creamed Corn 95

Excommomunicado Chocolate Pudding 97

Wick-y S'mores Dip 99

Hitman's style banana bread............................... 101

Assassin's Peach Cobbler 104

The Adjudicator's Style Meat Loaf............................. 106

Conclusion 108

Announcement.. 109

About the Author 10

Introduction

One interesting fact about movie characters is that they can be somewhat similar or totally different from the personality of the person playing them. First of all, everyone loves Keanu Reeves, but not because of the movies but because of the good he has done throughout his life and career. It's like he stands out among popular celebrities. He is the icon of our new world and everyone should take at least a fragment of his good deeds and implement them. The world would be a lot better place to live in.

John Wick, the name of the character that the movie was named after is also something that we can't resist. Not only because Keanu Reeves is there, but the plot, the twist that not many of us expected.

I was so into the movies that they inspired me to create one whole book with recipes.

The best thing about these recipes that are great for cooking for everyday lunch dinner and feel like you are eating out in a fancy restaurant.

Also if you are planning a family gathering or a small party, you'll find recipes here that will be easy to cook and fast so that you don't spend a lot of time in the kitchen.

Yes, I think about everything because I am like everyone else. I like to enjoy eating, but I want it to be simple and easy to make, so no matter if I am writing a book inspired by John Wick or others, I make sure everyone can do it.

Hot-Like-John Wings

Chicken wings are great but this recipe will turn your wings into a crowd pleaser easily.

List of Ingredients:

- 1 bottle hot pepper sauce
- 1 tsp. dried rosemary
- 1 tsp. dried thyme
- 2 pounds chicken wings
- 2 minced garlic cloves
- Salt and pepper

Procedure:

Cut chicken wings into small chunks and put in a bowl. Ass seasonings and hot pepper sauce to the bowl. Mix until chicken is evenly coated.

Transfer chicken to a greased baking dish.

Bake at 425° for about 40 minutes until chicken juices are clear.

Serve with desired dressing.

Wick-ed Tuna Casserole

Wicked because no matter how much of it you consume, it will always leave you begging for more.

List of Ingredients:

- 1/3 cup crushed cornflakes
- 1 package macaroni
- 1 can mushroom soup
- 1 cup sliced mushrooms
- 1 cup cheddar cheese
- 1 cup milk
- 1 can drained and flaked tuna
- 1 tsp. ground mustard
- 2 tbsp. diced pimientos
- 3 tsp. minced onion
- Salt

Procedure:

Cook macaroni according to instructions and drain.

Then combine the tuna, soup, milk, cheese, mushrooms, onion, pimentos, mustard and salt in a bowl.

Mix the soup and macaroni together thoroughly and sprinkle with cornflakes. Leave it uncovered.

Meanwhile, coat a baking dish with cooking spray.

Bake at 350° for about 30 minutes until it is bubbly.

The Elder's Potato Mash

Think of sloppy joes but with mash and spicy pies. That's what this recipe offers.

List of Ingredients:

- 1kg peeled and sliced sweet potatoes
- 1 tbsp. chilli powder
- 1 tbsp. ground cumin
- 1 tbsp. oil
- 1 tbsp. vegetable bouillon powder
- 2 sliced onions
- 2 tbsp. milk
- 50g finely grated cheddar
- 326g can of sweetcorn
- 400g can black-eyed beans
- 400g can chopped tomatoes
- 500g lean beef
- Pepper

Procedure:

Boil potato for 15 minutes or until softened. Mix the potatoes and milk to make a mash.

Heat oil in a pan over the medium heat. Add the onions and then cook for about 8 minutes or until softened.

Stir in the beef, bouillon, spices, beans and tomatoes. Allow to simmer for about 20 minutes.

Then add the corn with its water, add more spices. Stir the mixture, then remove the pan from heat.

Transfer the mince to a dish, top with mash and some cheese.

To eat it right away, heat it up in an oven to melt the cheese. Or freeze your pie until it is to be eaten.

Hitman's potato salad

Tweak your usual salad with this delicious potato salad recipe.

List of Ingredients:

- 1/2 cup sour cream
- 1 garlic clove
- 1 cup mayonnaise
- 1 tbsp. mustard
- 1 chopped onion
- 2 celery ribs
- 2 tbsp. minced parsley
- 3 pounds small red potatoes
- 6 boiled and sliced eggs
- Salt and pepper

Procedure:

Mix peeled garlic, potatoes, 1 tsp. salt and skewered garlic and water and allow it to boil.

Simmer for about 12 minutes or until potatoes are tender. Then drain potatoes.

Mix together sour cream, mustard, pepper, mayonnaise and salt. Whisk until thoroughly mixed.

Then stir in sliced eggs, potatoes, celery and onions. Refrigerate 4 hours.

Sprinkle with parsley and more sliced eggs before serving.

The Bogeyman's Brownies

Ever had brownies made with mashed potatoes? Well this recipe is your chance to try something new.

List of Ingredients:

- 1/3 cup cocoa powder
- 1/2 cup canola oil
- 1/2 cup flour
- 1/2 cup brown sugar
- 1/2 tsp. baking powder
- 3/4 cup mashed potatoes
- 1 tsp. vanilla extract
- 2 eggs
- Salt
- Sugar

Procedure:

Mix the mashed potatoes, vanilla, eggs, oil and sugar together in a bowl.

Add flour, baking powder, cocoa and salt to the mixture. Stir thoroughly then transfer the mixture to a greased baking pan.

Bake at 350° for about 30 minutes or until a knife inserted in the brownie comes out dry and clean.

Allow to cool and cut into slices to serve.

The Assassin's pie

This is a simple blueberry pie recipe that will take you back to grandma's kitchen.

List of Ingredients:

- 4 cups fresh blueberries
- 1 cup sugar
- Pastry for double-crust pie
- 2 tbsp. of butter
- 1 tbsp. of lemon juice
- Salt
- 1/4 cup tapioca

Procedure:

Roll dough on a flavoured surface then transfer to the pie plate. Leave it in refrigerator for 30 minutes.

Preheat oven to 400°. Mix the other ingredients - blueberries, salt, lemon juice, sugar and tapioca. Stir the mixture and let it sit for 15 minutes.

Place the filling on the baked pie and dot with butter. Reduce the heat to 350° and bake for 20 to 50 minutes on a lower oven rack, until the blueberries become bubbly.

Allow your pie to cool for about 4 hours before serving.

You can serve each slice of your Assassin's pie with whipped cream.

The Bowery King's Salmon Salad

Sumptuous salad recipe for all tastes.

List of Ingredients:

- 1/2 cup sour cream
- 1/4 cup chopped hazelnuts
- 1/4 cup fresh blueberries
- 1/4 cup finely chopped red pepper
- 1/4 cup snipped fresh dill
- 1 salmon fillet
- 1 cup chopped peeled cucumber
- 1 peeled and sliced peach
- 2 tbsp. lemon juice,
- 3 tbsp. capers
- 4 thin slices onion
- 8 cups torn lettuce
- Salt and pepper

Procedure:

Grease a baking sheet and place salmon on it. Sprinkle with pepper and salt, then pour 1 tbsp. lemon juice.

Bake at 425° for about 18 minutes or until the salmon chips. Cut the fish into large pieces.

Combine the salmon, lettuce, onion blueberries, hazelnut and peach in a bowl.

For dressing, mix sour cream, pepper, capers, lemon juice, snipped dill and cucumber in a bowl.

Serve the salad with dressing.

Bogeyman's style brisket

Brisket slices that tastes like heaven on a plate.

List of Ingredients:

- Fresh beef brisket
- Salt and pepper
- 5 cups wood chips
- Foil pan

Procedure:

Rub the brisket with salt and pepper, then place it in foil pan. Cover it up and leave it in the refrigerate overnight or for several hours.

Soak the wood chips in water, meanwhile prepare the grill for indirect and slow cooking.

Take your brisket out of the refrigerator and while still in the foil pan, place it on the grill rack and let the brisket cook.

Ensure that the grill temperature is at 275° all through the cooking.

Cook the brisket for about 4 hours or until meat is tender.

Then remove the brisket and let it cool for about 30 minutes.

To serve, unwrap the foil and cut the brisket into slices.

The Continental Pimiento Cheese Spread

Looking to try something different as topping for your hotdogs or sandwich spread. Here is a recipe for a spread you will fall on love with.

List of Ingredients:

- 1 cup shredded cheddar cheese
- 1 jar diced pimientos
- 1/3 cup mayonnaise

Procedure:

Mix mayonnaise, pimientos and cheese thoroughly. Refrigerate until chilled.

You can serve as spread for sandwiches and crackers or topping for hot dogs and hamburgers.

Wick-y Chicken

Ever wondered what type of chicken John would love? This chicken recipe may give you an idea.

List of Ingredients:

- 1 cup finely crushed cornflakes
- 1 egg
- 1 tbsp. milk
- 1/8 tsp. thyme leaves
- 2 tsp. butter
- 2 tsp. olive oil
- 4 chicken breast halves
- Salt and pepper

Procedure:

Preheat the oven to 425°.

Mix the egg and milk in one bowl. In another bowl, thoroughly mix the cornflake crumbs with salt, pepper and thyme.

Next, dip the chicken in the first mixture then coat it all over with the cornflake and spices mixture.

Using olive oil, grease up a baking sheet.

Place the chicken on the baking sheet then dot it with butter.

Put it in the oven and bake for about 20 minutes.

Wick Potatoes

An easy to fix potato recipe everyone in the family would love.

List of Ingredients:

- 2/3 cup buttermilk
- 1 cup sour cream
- 2 cups shredded cheddar cheese
- 2 tbsp. dried minced onion
- 4 pounds peeled potatoes
- Salt and pepper

Procedure:

Boil potatoes for about 15 minutes or until they are tender. Drain the water and grate the potatoes once they cool.

Mix the remaining ingredients in a bowl, add potatoes then stir until everything is thoroughly mixed.

Transfer the potatoes to a greased baking dish. Bake at 350° for about 40 minutes or until thoroughly heated.

Allow to cool before serving.

The High Table's Clam Chowder

A spoon of this thick and rich tasting soup will only leave you wanting more.

List of Ingredients:

- 1/8 tsp. dried thyme
- 1 chopped celery stalk
- 1 chopped onion
- 1 bottle clam juice
- 1 cup chicken broth
- 1 peeled and diced potato
- 2 cans chopped clams
- 2 cups heavy cream
- 3 tbsp. cornstarch
- Salt and pepper

Procedure:

Sauté celery and onion for about 4 minutes in a pot over medium heat.

Then add other ingredients - chicken broth, clam juice, clams, potatoes, pepper, salt and thyme. Cover the pot and allow to boil.

Boil for about 15 minutes or until the potatoes soften.

Mix your cornstarch in cream to dissolve it then add the mixture to your clam soup.

Stir frequently and allow the soup cook until you achieve your desired thickness.

Daisy's Special

A chili coney hot dog recipe that will have you begging for more.

List of Ingredients:

- 1/2 tsp. chili powder
- 1/2 tsp. garlic powder
- 1/2 tsp. ground mustard
- 1 can tomato sauce
- 1 pound lean ground beef
- 1 tbsp. dried minced onion
- 2 tbsp. Worcestershire sauce
- Hot dogs and hot dog buns
- Pepper
- Water

Procedure:

Cook beef over medium heat for about 7 minutes or until the meat is no longer pink. Drain the water and cut the meat into small chunks.

Stir in Worcestershire sauce, tomato sauce, seasonings and onion.

Place hot dogs on slow cooker and spoon the beef mixture on top. Cook for about 5 hours or until the hotdog is thoroughly heated.

Serve on buns with your desired toppings.

The Adjudicator's pudding

Amazing baked rice pudding recipe that introduces another level of sweetness and texture to the dessert casserole.

List of Ingredients:

- 1/2 cup honey
- 1 cup raisins
- 2 cups cooked rice
- 3 cups milk
- 3 eggs

Procedure:

Preheat the oven to 350°.

Mix the ingredients - rice, honey, milk, eggs and raisins in a bowl.

Grease a baking dish and place the mixture in it.

Allow the rice bake for up to 1 hour or until the colour is golden.

Remove it from the oven and allow to cool.

You can serve your Adjudicator's pudding with cream for extra flavour.

Sweet Like John Cream Pie

There is absolutely everything to love about sugar cream pie, especially if you are using this recipe.

List of Ingredients:

- 1/4 cup cornstarch
- 1/4 tsp. ground cinnamon
- 1/2 cup butter
- 1 cup sugar
- 1 tsp. vanilla extract
- 2 cups milk
- Pastry for single-crust pie

Procedure:

Preheat oven to 450°.

Roll dough and fit the crust in a pie plate. Flute the edge. Line the crust with a thick. Fill with uncooked rice, dried beans and pie weights.

Bake for 15 minutes or until light brown.

Meanwhile, mix cornstarch and sugar in another pan, add milk and stir until smooth. Allow to cook for 2 minutes or until bubbly and thickened.

Remove from heat, add vanilla and butter, spoon it to the crust and sprinkle with cinnamon.

Bake for about 20 minutes or until light golden.

Allow to cool then refrigerate until ready to serve.

Wick's Casserole

Bake up Cheese Steak Casserole using this delicious recipe and watch everyone race to the table.

List of Ingredients:

- 1 thinly sliced onion
- Thinly sliced beef sirloin steak,
- Cooked noodles
- 1 tbsp. vegetable oil
- 1 jar cheese sauce
- 2 sliced red peppers
- Salt and pepper

Procedure:

Preheat oven to 350°

Place the cooked noodles in a baking dish with cooking spray. Then put it aside.

Add pepper and onion in a skillet and sauté for about 5 minutes over low heat.

Add salt, pepper and beef to the mixture and stir occasionally. Cook for 4 minutes then drain the liquid.

Melt cheese sauce then scoop the cheese and place it over noodles. Place beef mixture on the cheese sauce then top the beef mixture with cheese sauce.

Cover up your dish with foil and bake for 30 minutes.

Remove from the oven when it is thoroughly heated and allow to cool before serving.

Baba Yaga's Collard Greene

Looking to try out a new side dish. This collard greens with bacon recipe will appeal to your taste buds.

List of Ingredients:

- 1/2 tsp. garlic powder
- 1 cup chopped onion
- 1 cup dried and chopped tomatoes
- 2 pounds collard greens
- 4 bacon strips
- 5 cups chicken broth
- Salt and red pepper flakes

Procedure:

Trim the stems of the greens and cup the leaves.

Sauté bacon and onion for about 12 minutes or until bacon is crisp and onion is tender. Add greens and cook until tender.

Add other ingredients and allow the mixture to simmer for about 50 minutes.

Remove from heat and allow to cool before serving.

Wick and beans

This beans recipe is awesome and will be a big hit in every picnic or barbecue.

Ingredient

- 1/2 cup chopped onion
- 1/2 pound ground beef
- 1/3 cup packed brown sugar
- 1/4 cup barbecue sauce
- 1/4 cup ketchup
- 1/4 cup maple syrup
- 2 tbsp. molasses
- 2 tbsp. mustard
- 2 cans of beans
- Salt and pepper

Procedure:

Preheat oven to 350°.

Cook onion and beef in a skillet over medium heat. Then drain the water.

Add maple syrup, barbecue sauce, mustard, ketchup, salt, chili powder and other ingredients to the skillet.

Add the beans and stir.

Transfer the mixture to a greased baking dish and bake for about 1 hour.

The High Table Chicken Enchilada Casserole

Everyone at the table will gobble up this dish before you can say mini marshmallow.

List of Ingredients:

- 1 can green enchilada sauce
- 1 cup sour cream
- 4 cups shredded rotisserie chicken
- 4 cups shredded cheese
- 9 corn tortillas cut into small pieces

Procedure:

Preheat oven to 375°.

Grease the baking dish and then add the following in layers to the dish chicken, sour cream, cheese, enchilada sauce and tortillas.

Cover it up and allow to bake for about 50 minutes or until bubbly.

Let it cool for about 10 minutes before serving.

Baba Yaga's Rice

When it comes to colourful dishes, it doesn't get much better than this mouth-watering rice recipe.

List of Ingredients:

- 1/8 tsp. ground turmeric
- 1 tbsp. olive oil
- 1 diced green pepper
- 1 chopped onion
- 1 cup rice
- 1 can black beans
- 1 can chicken broth
- 2 cups frozen corn
- 2 garlic cloves
- Diced tomatoes

Procedure:

Sauté onion, pepper and garlic in oil over medium to high heat. Allow to cook for 3 minutes.

Then add spices, rice and broth. Cover the pot and allow it to boil for about 15 minutes until the rice is soft.

Add the other ingredients and cook until rice is thoroughly heated.

The Continental Fried Okra

Your recipe for the ultimate crunchy and appetizing okra nuggets.

List of Ingredients:

- 1/4 tsp. seasoning blend
- 1 cup sliced fresh okra
- 2 tbsp. flour
- 42. 2 tbsp. cornmeal
- 3 tbsp. buttermilk
- Salt and pepper
- Oil

Procedure:

Mix flour, salt, pepper and seasoning blend in a bowl.

Pour buttermilk in another bowl then dip the dry okra in it.

Roll the now wet okra in the cornmeal mixture until fully coated.

Heat oil in a skillet at 375°. Fry each okra in the oil for about 2 minutes or until both sides are until golden brown.

Drain off excess oil. Can serve with extra seasoning if desired.

John's Hash

Learn how to prepare your hash in a different way using this delicious hash recipe

List of Ingredients:

- 1 cup tomato sauce
- 1 tbsp. hot sauce
- 1 tbsp. vegetable oil
- 1 thinly sliced onion
- 1 thinly sliced red bell pepper,
- Corned beef
- Peeled and diced potatoes
- Salt and pepper
- 4 garlic cloves
- 6 eggs

Procedure:

Heat oil in a skillet. Add potatoes and cook over medium heat, stirring occasionally. Cook for about 10 minutes or until the colour is golden.

Season with salt, pepper and onion. Cook over medium heat for about 2 minutes.

Stir in the corned beef and cook for about 8 minutes. Then add the tomato sauce, garlic and add 1 tbsp. of hot sauce. Cook for about 15 minutes until you achieve a thick consistency with the sauce.

In another skillet, fry your eggs sunny side up.

Serve the hash topped with the eggs.

Bowery King's Gelatin Salad

A blueberry salad recipe like no other.

List of Ingredients:

- 1/2 cup sugar
- 1/2 cup chopped walnuts
- 1 can blueberry pie filling
- 1 can crushed pineapple
- 1 cup sour cream
- 1 package softened cream cheese
- 1 tsp. vanilla extract
- 2 cups hot water
- 2 packages grape gelatin

Procedure:

Dissolve gelatin in the hot water then allow to cool for about 10 minutes. Stir in pineapple and pie filling until it is well mixed.

Transfer to a dish, cover it up and refrigerate for about 1 hour.

To make topping, combine vanilla, sugar, sour cream and cream cheese in a bowl. Spread over gelatin and top with walnuts.

Refrigerate until firm.

The Hitman's Chicken Enchiladas

Delicious chicken enchiladas you won't be able to get enough of.

List of Ingredients:

- 1 can black beans
- 1 chopped tomato
- 1 cup shredded cooked rotisserie chicken
- 1 jar salsa
- 2 cups grated cheese
- 3 corn tortillas
- Salt and Pepper
- Sour cream

Procedure:

Preheat oven to 175°C.

Season chicken with pepper and salt then put it aside.

Spread salsa around your baking dish

Then pour a mixture of your seasoned chicken, tomatoes, beans and cheese into tortillas.

Roll up the tortillas and place them in baking dish. Top tortillas in the dish with more cheese and salsa.

Allow to bake for about 30 minutes.

You can serve the Enchiladas with sour cream.

Wick's Brunswick Stew

Colourful stew recipe packed with a combo of veggies and chicken.

List of Ingredients:

- 1/4 cup butter
- 1/2 cup dry breadcrumbs
- 1 can corn
- 1 can diced tomatoes
- 1 can beans
- 1 cut up broiler chicken
- 2 sliced onions
- 4 peeled and cubed potatoes
- Salt and pepper
- Water

Procedure:

Boil chicken in water and allow to simmer or about 60 minutes or until softened.

Transfer the chicken to a bowl and cube it up. Then return to broth.

Add potatoes, beans, onion and spices to the broth and boil. Allow to simmer for about 30 minutes or until potatoes are soft.

Add the remaining ingredients and boil for 10 minutes until thickened.

Heavy Duty Ham

Imagine ham that can be frozen for several weeks then thawed and eaten like nothing happened. Well this recipe isn't called heavy duty ham for nothing.

List of Ingredients:

- Whole cloves
- Cooked ham
- 1 cup orange marmalade
- 1 cup orange soda
- 1/4 cup mustard
- 1/2 cup brown sugar

Procedure:

Preheat oven to 325°.

Put ham on a rack in a roasting pan, then make shapes on the surface of the ham where you will insert cloves.

Cover up the ham with foil and bake for about 90 minutes.

Mix the brown sugar, marmalade and soda in a saucepan, then boil for about 15 minutes. Stir in the mustard after a while.

Brush up the ham with the sauce, then let it bake for another 20 minutes. Brush it up with the glaze occasionally.

Let it cool for about 10 minutes before you slice it up and serve.

The Adjudicator Style Cobbler

Ever had crumpled macaroon toppings on rhubarb cobbler? This recipe is your chance.

List of Ingredients:

- 1/2 cup brown sugar
- 1/2 tsp. ground cinnamon
- 1 peeled and sliced apple
- 1 tbsp. cornstarch
- 1 tbsp. melted butter
- 2 tbsp. sugar
- 4 cups sliced fresh rhubarb
- 8 crumbled macaroons
- Cold water

Procedure:

Mix apple, rhubarb, cinnamon and sugar together in a skillet. Simmer for about 10 minutes until rhubarb is tender.

Add water and cornstarch and mix until smooth. Stir in the fruit and allow to boil for about 2 minutes until thickened.

Mix sugar, butter, cookies and cinnamon in a bowl. Then sprinkle over fruit mixture.

Boil for 5 minutes until golden. Serve warm if desired.

The Elder's Macaroni and Cheese

This is not your regular macaroni and cheese recipe, the added spices and herbs brings a new dimension to it.

List of Ingredients:

- 1/2 tsp. seasoning
- 1/4 cup sour cream
- 1/4 tsp. onion powder
- 3/4 cup shredded cheddar cheese
- 1 package uncooked macaroni
- 1 cup milk
- 2 tbsp. butter
- 2 tbsp. flour
- 2 tbsp. grated cheese
- 2 tbsp. seasoned breadcrumbs
- Salt and pepper

Procedure:

Cook macaroni according to instructions then put it in a bowl and set aside.

Pour butter in a pan and melt over medium heat, then add seasoning, flour and milk. Allow it to cook for 2 minutes. Stir occasionally until it is thickened.

Remove the saucepan from heat, add cheese and sour cream. Stir until the cheese is fully melted.

Coat macaroni with the sauce. Then sprinkle breadcrumbs and more cheese on the casserole.

Bake it at 350° for about 20 minutes until the dish is thoroughly heated.

Hitman's Hash

Enjoy the classic hash dish with extra flavour using this east to make recipe.

List of Ingredients:

- 3/4 cup half-and-half cream
- 1/2 pound turkey pastrami
- 1 cup diced beets
- 1 onion
- 1 tbsp. canola oil
- 1 tsp. hot sauce
- 1 tbsp. minced fresh parsley
- 3 cups cubed hash brown potatoes
- Salt and pepper

Procedure:

Mix salt, pepper, onion hot sauce and cream together in a bowl. Cook until tender for about 3 minutes.

Stir in potatoes, beets and pastrami. Cook for about 10 minutes or until thoroughly heated. Remove from heat.

Spoon hash to a plate and sprinkle with parsley.

Fry eggs sunny side up and serve with hash.

Continental Hotel Apple Pie

While this might seem like a regular apple pie, the filling makes all the difference.

List of Ingredients:

- 1/2 cup sugar
- 1/4 tsp. ground nutmeg
- 1/8 tsp. ground ginger
- 1 tsp. ground cinnamon
- 1 tbsp. lemon juice
- 2 tbsp. water
- 3 tbsp. flour
- 6 cups sliced peeled tart apples
- Salt
- Pastry for double-crust pie

Procedure:

Mix apples with lemon juice and water in a pan. Cook over medium heat until the apples are softened. Remove the pan from the heat and set it aside.

Then mix the flour, sugar, cinnamon, ginger, salt and nutmeg in q bowl. Pour in your apples and mix.

Place the apple mixture in between top and bottom crusts of pastry.

Seal the edges of the pastry and make slits on the top crust. Allow to bake at 400° for about 40 minutes or until the pie is golden brown.

Excommomunicado Jambalaya

Enjoy a variant of the Jambalaya dish with this delicious recipe.

List of Ingredients:

- 1/2 cup chopped celery
- 1/2 tsp. chili powder
- 1/4 tsp. pepper
- 1/4 cup chopped green pepper
- 3/4 cup chopped onion
- 1 can diced tomatoes
- 1 can condensed beef broth
- 1 cup uncooked white rice
- 1 pounds peeled and deveined uncooked shrimp
- 1 tsp. sugar
- 1 tsp. dried thyme
- 1 tbsp. minced fresh parsley
- 2 tbsp. butter
- 2 garlic cloves
- 2 cups cubed cooked ham
- Water

Procedure:

Sauté pepper, celery, garlic and onion in butter over medium heat. Cook for 1 minute.

The other ingredients except parsley and shrimp and cook for about 25 minutes until rice is tender.

Add parsley and shrimp, allow to simmer for 10 minutes until shrimp is pink.

John's Sloppy Joes

A mix of fresh veggies and earthly spices bring a new dimension to your traditional sloppy Joes.

List of Ingredients:

- 1/8 tsp. black pepper
- 1/8 tsp. cinnamon
- 1/2 cup grated cheese
- 1/2 cup sour cream
- 1 can tomato paste
- 1 clove garlic
- 1 red bell pepper
- 1 pound ground beef
- 1 small onion
- 1 tsp. cumin
- 1 tbsp. olive oil
- 4 toasted hamburger buns
- Salt and pepper

Procedure:

Heat the oil over medium heat in a pan.

Add garlic, pepper and onion to the pan and sauté for 3 minutes. Add the beef and cook for 5 more minutes.

Add the pepper, salt, cinnamon, chilli powder and tomato paste. Stir occasionally. Allow to simmer for about 12 minutes or until thickened.

Place the mixture on the buns, then top with sour cream and cheddar.

Wick Style Cheese Soup

Ever had cheese soup mixed with beer? No? Well this is your chance.

List of Ingredients:

- 1/2 cup flour
- 1/2 cup water
- 1 finely chopped small onion
- 3 finely chopped medium carrots
- 3 tbsp. butter
- 4 cups fresh broccoli florets
- 4 cans chicken broth
- 5 finely chopped celery ribs
- 1 package cream cheese
- 1 bottle beer
- Pepper

Procedure:

Mix carrots, celery and onion, then sauté in melted butter over medium heat. Cook until it is tender.

Then add broccoli, pepper, broth, flour and water. Allow to boil for about 30 minutes, stirring occasionally until the vegetables are soft and the soup is thickened.

Stir in beer and cheese until the cheese completely melts into the soup.

Add toppings like green onions, bacon, croutons and sour cream.

Bogeyman's Buckeye

Chocolate peanut butter covered balls? Yes please.

List of Ingredients:

- 1 cup butter
- 1 cup peanut butter
- 1 tsp. shortening
- 4 cups chocolate chips
- 5 cup sugar

Procedure:

Beat peanut butter, sugar and butter in a bowl until thoroughly mixed. Shape into small balls and put aside.

Microwave chocolate chips until melted then stir until smooth. Insert balls in chocolate and refrigerate for 15 minutes or until firm.

Store in the refrigerator until ready to serve.

Wick n Peas

Need an alternative to regular salads? Well say hello to the Wick n Pea salad with this recipe.

List of Ingredients:

- 1/2 cup mayonnaise
- 1/4 cup salad dressing
- 1/4 cup chopped red onion
- 2 cups frozen peas
- 1 cup chopped celery
- 1 cup dry roasted peanuts
- Cooked and crumbled bacon strips

Procedure:

Mix the peas, peanuts, celery bacon strips and onion in a bowl.

Add salad dressing and mayonnaise to the bowl and stir into salad.

Cover it up and refrigerate for about 4 hours, before serving.

The High Table Potato Salad

A type of recipe that promises no leftovers.

List of Ingredients:

- 1/2 pound sliced bacon
- 3/4 tsp. ground mustard
- 1 cup thinly sliced celery
- 1 cup chopped onion
- 1 cup sugar
- 1 cup cider vinegar
- 1 tsp. salt
- 2 tbsp. all-purpose flour
- 2 medium carrots
- 2 tbsp. minced fresh parsley
- 5 pounds cooked small red potatoes
- Water

Procedure:

Cook bacon in a pan over medium heat until it is crisp.

Then remove the bacon to a bowl.

Drain the dripping, leaving some to sauté onion and celery until it is soft.

Mix the flour, sugar, vinegar, mustard and water. Add to the pan and allow to boil for about 2 minutes. Stir continuously.

Mix the potatoes, parsley and carrots. Drizzle with sauce and turn around to coat.

Crumble bacon on salad and eat warm.

Baba Yaga's noodle soup

Chicken noodle soup is the go to soup on cold winter days. Here's a recipe to try out when winter comes around again.

List of Ingredients:

- Salt and Pepper
- 1 chopped onion
- 1 minced garlic clove
- 1 tbsp. fresh parsley
- 1 tbsp. lemon juice
- 1 tbsp. canola oil
- 1/4 tsp. dried thyme
- 2 bay leaves
- 2 pounds skinless chicken thighs
- 3 cups uncooked egg noodles
- 4 chopped celery ribs
- 4 chopped carrots
- 10 cups chicken broth

Procedure:

Season chicken with salt and pepper and cook in oil over medium heat.

Cook for about 4 minutes or until the chicken has a golden or brown colour. Then remove chicken from pan.

Add onion and garlic to the pan with the drippings, stir occasionally. Cook for 5 minutes or until tender.

Stir in broth and allow to boil.

Return the chicken to pan, then add carrots, bay leaves, thyme and celery. Simmer for 30 minutes or until chicken is tender.

Remove the pan from heat and put the chicken in a plate. Then add noodles to the soup, cover and let it stand for about 30 minutes or until they soften.

Shred the chicken into small bits, add it to the noodles pot. Stir in lemon juice, parsley and more seasoning for extra flavour.

John's Okra and Chicken Gumbo

A creole dish you will never forget.

List of Ingredients:

- 1/4 cup canola oil
- 1 can tomatoes
- 1 chopped green pepper
- 1 tsp. dried basil
- 1 fryer chicken
- 2 bay leaves
- 2 cups fresh sliced okra
- 2 chopped celery ribs
- 2 chopped onions
- 2 quarts water
- 2 tbsp. flour
- 2 tsp. hot pepper sauce
- 2 tbsp. sliced green onions
- 3 garlic cloves
- Minced fresh parsley
- Cooked rice
- Salt and pepper

Procedure:

Boil chicken for about 40 minutes or until chicken is tender. Then set it aside and reserve broth.

Cut the chicken into cubes and put aside.

Mix oil and flour thoroughly, then cook over medium heat for about 5 minutes, stirring constantly.

Add broth and boil. Stir continuously until thickened for 2 minutes.

Add the remaining ingredients and chicken allow to simmer for 1 hour.

Add chicken and allow to heat thoroughly.

Garnish with parsley and green onions.

The Bogeyman's Funeral Potatoes

They may be dubbed funeral potatoes but this recipe can make you feel alive like never before.

List of Ingredients:

- 1/2 cup diced onion
- 1 can cream of celery soup
- 1 cup crushed crackers
- 1 package shredded hash browns
- 1 stick butter
- 2 cups shredded cheese
- 2 cups sour cream
- Salt and pepper

Procedure:

Preheat oven to 375°. Meanwhile coat baking dish with cooking spray.

Melt butter in a pan over medium heat. Add onion and sauté until soft.

Mix the soup, cheese, hash browns, salt, pepper and sour cream in a bowl. Then transfer the mixture to sprayed baking dish.

Melt butter and add cracker crumbs then mix it thoroughly. Brush the cracker mixture on potatoes and foil the baking dish.

Bake for 35 minutes with foil and 15 minutes without the foil covering. Remove baking dish from microwave when the potatoes are golden brown.

Parabellum-Style Ribs

Enjoy these amazing ribs recipe for a taste of perfection.

List of Ingredients:

- 1/4 cup ketchup
- 1/4 cup molasses
- 1/4 tsp. smoked paprika
- 1/4 tsp. cayenne pepper
- 1 cup brown sugar
- 1 cup tomato sauce
- 1 finely chopped onion
- 1 tbsp. apple cider vinegar
- 1 tsp. ground mustard
- 2 tsp. garlic powder
- 2 tbsp. canola oil
- 2 tsp. Worcestershire sauce
- 12 country-style pork ribs

Procedure:

Mix seasonings and brown sugar. Sprinkle on ribs, cover and refrigerate for about an hour.

For sauce, heat oil over medium heat and add onion. Cook for about 6 minutes until softened.

Stir in other ingredients and allow to boil. Then remove pan from heat.

Wrap ribs in foil and grill over indirect medium heat for about 90 minutes or until ribs are tender.

Remove ribs from foil and coat with sauce. Grill for about 10 minutes turning occasionally until the ribs are browned.

The Continental Onion Dip

Looking for an easy to make and delicious party food? This onion dip recipe is your answer

List of Ingredients:

- 1 container sour cream
- 1 ripe mashed avocado
- 1 envelope onion soup mix

Procedure:

Add onion soup mix, avocado and sour cream to a bowl and mix thoroughly.

Cover it up and refrigerate for about 2 hours before serving.

The Continental Salad

What do you get when you mix avocado, tomato and corn salad with roast chicken and buttermilk dressing? The Continental style Salad.

List of Ingredients:

- 1 lime
- 2 corn cobs
- 2 ripe avocados
- 2 spring onions
- 2 tbsp. milk
- 2 tbsp. olive oil
- 125g coarse bread
- 600g sliced tomatoes
- 115g mayonnaise
- Mustard
- 1 garlic clove
- 125ml buttermilk

Procedure:

Tear up the bread and soak in a bowl with water and milk. Soak for 20 minutes then take out the bread and squeeze out some liquid.

Heat up oil in a pan and cook the bread over medium heat. Add seasoning and turn the bread occasionally. Cook until the bread is thoroughly heated, crisp and golden brown.

Cut off the corn kernels and put in a bowl with oil. Add a little seasoning.

Let it roast in the oven for about 20 minutes. Toss occasionally.

For the dressing, put garlic, mustard, chives and mayonnaise in a bowl. Then stir in the buttermilk until there are no lumps left.

Slice up the avocados and squeeze the lime juice on them.

Add other salad dressing **List of Ingredients:** and mix together.

Spoon the dressing over and serve others on the side.

Bowery King's Stuffed Salmon

Experience seafood like never before with this crab meat stuffed salmon recipe.

List of Ingredients:

- 1/4 cup melted butter
- 1/4 tsp. garlic powder
- 1/2 cup breadcrumbs
- 1/2 pound flakes crabmeat
- 1/2 tsp. onion powder
- 1 tsp. chopped parsley
- 6 salmon fillets

Procedure:

Preheat oven to 350°. Meanwhile coat a baking sheet with cooking spray.

Except the salmon, mix other ingredients together in a bowl and set it aside.

Cut a slit through the salmon fillet, about 3/4 of its length. Then put the stuffing in the slit of each salmon and transfer the fish to the prepared baking sheet.

Bake for about 20 minutes or until the fish chips.

Baba Yaga's Creamed Corn

Need a side dish that goes with basically anything? This creamy cheesy recipe will not disappoint you.

List of Ingredients:

- 1 finely chopped onion
- 1 tbsp. sugar
- 3 corn cobs
- 75g butter
- 125ml single cream
- Mozzarella

Procedure:

Heat up butter in a pan, add onion and sauté for about 5 minutes.

Add the corn kernels to the pan then add water. Cook over medium heat for 10 minutes.

Then add sugar, cream and seasoning. Cook for 5 more minutes.

Sprinkle with mozzarella and cook for 2 more minutes or until melted.

Excommomunicado Chocolate Pudding

Want to try out something different for dessert, here's a chocolate pudding recipe even the pickiest of tastes would love.

List of Ingredients:

- 1 cup whipped topping
- 1 cup cold chocolate pudding
- 2 tsp. cold hazelnut coffee creamer
- 2 tsp. sliced almonds

Procedure:

Mix the coffee creamer and whipped topping thoroughly in a bowl

Distribute the chocolate pudding in small shot glasses in your preferred quantity. Then top with 2 layers of more whipped topped.

Sprinkle almonds on top of each glass.

Keep it refrigerated until you are ready to serve.

Wick-y S'mores Dip

The chocolatey twist in this s'mores dip recipe will have everyone camping in your kitchen.

List of Ingredients:

- 200g milk chocolate
- 350g mini marshmallows
- 2 tbsp. milk
- 100g biscuits
- 100g strawberries
- 100g pineapple

Procedure:

Heat the milk, chocolate and half of the marshmallows in a pan over medium heat. Cook until the mixture is smooth and melted.

Top the cream with the remaining marshmallows until the entire surface is covered.

Grill for about 2 minutes or until the marshmallows are brown. Serve with pineapples, strawberries and biscuits.

Hitman's style banana bread

This is not your regular banana bread recipe. This special pineapple banana bread will have everyone racing to the table.

List of Ingredients:

- 1/2 cup sugar
- 1 can crushed pineapple
- 1 cup vegetable oil
- 1 cup chopped macadamia nuts
- 1 tsp. baking soda
- 1 tsp. ground cinnamon
- 2 cups mashed ripe bananas
- 2 tsp. vanilla extract
- 2 cups sugar
- 3 cups flour
- Salt
- 3 eggs

Procedure:

Preheat oven to 350°. Then prepare your loaf pans, first coat with cooking spray, next, dust with flour.

Mix the dry **List of Ingredients:**- flour, baking soda, sugar, salt and cinnamon in one bowl. Then add macadamia nuts.

Mix the wet ingredients in another bowl and stir thoroughly.

Pour the wet into the dry mixture and stir until both mixtures are thoroughly combined.

Transfer the batter to the prepared loaf pans.

Bake for about 90 minutes or until a small knife inserted through the centre of the loaf comes out dry and clean.

Remove bread from oven and let it cool for about 10 minutes.

Mix your pineapple liquid with sugar and drizzle it over the cooled banana bread loaf.

Assassin's Peach Cobbler

Give your peach cobbler a new look with fluffy biscuits.

List of Ingredients:

- 1/2 cup sugar
- 2/3 cup heavy cream
- 1 tsp. baking powder
- 1 cup flour
- 6 tbsp. unsalted butter
- 8 chopped peaches
- Vanilla ice cream

Procedure:

Preheat oven to 350°. Meanwhile, dust baking dish with flour.

Combine the peaches with some sugar, and some flour then mix thoroughly.

Mix the remaining flour with sugar, butter, salt and baking powder. Stir until the dough forms coarse crumbs form. Then add cream and continue to stir until the dough is moistened.

Spoon the batter on top of the peaches.

Bake for about 60 minutes until golden brown.

You can serve your peach cobbler with vanilla ice cream.

The Adjudicator's Style Meat Loaf

Ever had a meat loaf with bacon, well here's your chance thanks to this mouth-watering recipe.

List of Ingredients:

- 1/2 cup milk
- 1/2 cup tomato sauce
- 1/2 tsp. ground cumin
- 1/4 tsp. ground nutmeg
- 1 cup breadcrumbs
- 1 celery stalk
- 1 onion
- 1 tbsp. olive oil
- 2 eggs
- 2 garlic cloves
- 2 pounds meat-loaf mix
- 4 strips sliced bacon
- Salt and pepper

Procedure:

Preheat oven to 350°.

Heat oil in a skillet, over medium heat. Then add celery, onion, jalapeño and garlic. Cook for about 10 minutes until the vegetables are tender.

Add salt, nutmeg and cumin. Then remove the pan from heat.

Whisk the eggs in a bowl then stir in milk, breadcrumbs and tomato sauce.

Add the cooked vegetables and meat to the egg bowl.

Transfer the mixture to a loaf pan. Top the loaf with bacon strips cut in half and tuck in the ends.

Bake for about 15 minutes.

Let it cool for 10 minutes before serving.

Conclusion

And there you have it 50 mouth watering John Wick inspired dishes. We assure you these recipes will be loved everywhere and across all ages. These meals will make a nice addition to your menu if you are looking for amazing recipes to try out.

Announcement

Thank you

Thank you very much for getting this book. By buying my book you show me that you are ready to learn new skills and I can tell for sure you have made the best decision. I become a recipe writer because I love to share my knowledge and experience so that other people can learn.

What's even more special is that from all the books that are available on the internet today you have mine. With every purchase done it's like a gift to me, proof that I've made the best decision, turning my experience and knowledge into a book.

Still, please do not forget to leave feedback after reading the book. This is very important for me because I'll know how far I have reached. Even if you have any suggestions that you think it will make my future books even more practice please do share. Plus, everyone else that won't be able to decide which book to get next will have real feedback to read.

Thank you again

Your truly

Betty Green

About the Author

The one thing she loves more than cooking is eating. Yes, Betty Green enjoys tasting new dishes and loves to experiment with food. While sticking to the classics is also a thing, she wants to create recipes that people can enjoy daily.

She really understands the struggle of choosing the next lunch or dinner or what they should serve at their parties. So, she makes sure that her recipes are not only great for family dinners, or even a single dish but for parties too.

She always says "I have a strong sense of smell and taste, which gives me an advantage in creating new recipes from scratch".

The best part of Betty's recipes is that they are practical and very easy to make. When she does use ingredients that are not so easy to find or rarely used in cooking she makes sure to explain everything and add a simplified cooking description so that everyone can make them.

Everyone who got a cookbook from her says that she changed their life. Helped them finally enjoy spending time in the kitchen, which even helped them bond stronger with their family and friends.

Well, after all, food is one of the best ways to connect with people whether they make the dish together or they sit down and eat it. There are countless ways food can help you in your life, aside from keeping you fed and healthy.

Manufactured by Amazon.ca
Bolton, ON

29475452R00061